THE BIBLE STUDY GUIDE FOR BEGINNERS

THE
OLD TESTAMENT

JOSEPH KNOWLE

DEDICATION

This book is dedicated to all of those who thirst for knowledge.
It is also dedicated to my family – may you continue to learn and grow.

Contents

JOSEPH KNOWLE

Introduction

Thank you for purchasing this book. I hope that you find God's guidance through each of the 39 chapters in the Old Testament, and deepen your relationship with God while doing so.

THE OLD TESTAMENT

Genesis

Author: Moses

Time Period: Before 4000 BC   1806 BC

Key Themes / Outline: Narrative History. Creation. Adam, Eve, Noah, Abraham, Sarah, Isaac, Rebekah, Jacob, and Joseph. Rebellion against God. God choosing the Israelites.

Summary of the message:

Genesis is the first book of the bible and was written to record God's creation of the world and to demonstrate His love for all that He created. It is also the first book of Law.

The name Genesis means *"In the Beginning"*. It explains the events of the origin of life. Genesis describes God creating everything by the power of His spoken Word.

Due to sin in the world, introduced by Adam and Eve eating the forbidden fruit, God implements judgement by the way of a universal flood, but spares Noah, a faithful man, and his family. Humanity is wiped out with exception for this one chosen family.

God has a plan for redemption, creating His own nation of Israel. God chooses Abraham, another faithful man, and promises to bless him with a multitude of people with which to bless the world. Abraham and his family are blessed by God, and even though they go through trials, The Lord displays His power. By the end of Genesis, God's people are in a foreign land, and are forward to the promised land.

Scripture to reflect on:

Genesis 1:1 'In the beginning God created the heavens and the earth'

Exodus

Author: Moses

Time Period: 1800 BC – 1445 BC

Key Themes / Outline: narrative, and Laws. God rescuing the Israelites from slavery. Moses and the laws to govern a new nation.

Summary of the message:

Exodus is a written record of the events of Israel's deliverance from slavery in Egypt. It also lists the Laws that God has given to the Israelites, as a set of rules to develop a relationship with God.

Moses is introduced as a baby whose life is spared, and then adopted by Pharaoh's daughter and raised as an Egyptian. God reveals himself to Moses through a burning bush, and calls him to release His people from slavery in Egypt. Moses obeys, and he and his brother Aaron confront Pharaoh. Pharaoh ignores the plea.

God releases 10 different types of plagues on the land of Egypt, which ends with the death of every first born son, sparing those of Gods people. After the death of Pharaohs son, Pharaoh can take no more and allows them to go.

Moses escapes with his people and makes it to the Red Sea. Pharaoh changes his mind, and goes after them. Moses, with the power of God, parts the Red Sea, allowing his people through, and closing it to kill Pharaoh's army as the sea closed.

Moses presents the Ten Commandments at Mt. Sinai, and gives the

Israelites the tabernacle, priest and worship directives.

Scripture to reflect on:

Exodus 20:1-17

The Ten Commandments

20 And God spoke all these words:

> ² "I am the LORD your God, who brought you out of Egypt, out of the land of slavery.

³ "You shall have no other gods before[a] me.

⁴ "You shall not make for yourself an image in the form of anything in heaven above or on the earth beneath or in the waters below. ⁵ You shall not bow down to them or worship them; for I, the LORD your God, am a jealous God, punishing the children for the sin of the parents to the third and fourth generation of those who hate me, ⁶ but showing love to a thousand generations of those who love me and keep my commandments.

⁷ "You shall not misuse the name of the LORD your God, for the LORD will not hold anyone guiltless who misuses his name.

⁸ "Remember the Sabbath day by keeping it holy. ⁹ Six days you shall labor and do all your work, ¹⁰ but the seventh day is a Sabbath to the LORD your God. On it you shall not do any work, neither you, nor your son or daughter, nor your male or female servant, nor your animals, nor any foreigner

residing in your towns. ¹¹ For in six days the LORD made the heavens and the earth, the sea, and all that is in them, but he rested on the seventh day. Therefore, the LORD blessed the Sabbath day and made it holy.

¹² "Honor your father and your mother, so that you may live long in the land the LORD your God is giving you.

¹³ "You shall not murder.

¹⁴ "You shall not commit adultery.

¹⁵ "You shall not steal.

¹⁶ "You shall not give false testimony against your neighbor.

¹⁷ "You shall not covet your neighbor's house. You shall not covet your neighbor's wife, or his male or female servant, his ox or donkey, or anything that belongs to your neighbor."

Leviticus

Author: Moses

Time Period: 1445 BC

Key Themes / Outline: Narrative History and Law. The laws regarding being holy and worshipping God.

Summary of the message:

This book draws to the attention of the Israelites the infinite holiness of God, and that they are to act in a holy way, particularly towards Him. It includes laws for living a holy life.

Leviticus is set mostly in Mt Sinai, where Moses instructions on the procedures for things that are unclean, and the importance of these procedures in protecting Gods people from illnesses and diseases. These include food, diseases, animals, insects, dead bodies, birth, cleaning and many others. pertain to the laws that apply generally for living a holy life.

It also covers sacrifices to be made, for Gods redemption of the Israelites ungodliness.

Scripture to reflect on:

Leviticus 26:3-4

3. If you follow my decrees and are careful to obey my commands

4 I will send you rain in its season, and the ground will yield its crops

and the trees of the field their fruit.

Numbers

Author: Moses

Time Period: 1445 BC – 1407 BC

Key Themes / Outline: Narrative. Due to rebellion, the Israelites had to wander through the wilderness for forty years before being delivered to the promised land.

Summary of the message:

Numbers is written to detail the preparation taken by the Israelites before entering the promised land.

Moses takes a census of the population, thus the name Numbers.

The Israelites travel from the wilderness on their journey to the promised land, complaining along the way about their food. God gives them Quail. Due to their greed, God also sends a plague. There is further punishment for unfaithfulness.

12 spies are sent into the promised land in preparation, and after returning with good news, the Israelites get scared and rebel against the move. God sends further punishment, and sends the Israelites back in to the wilderness for forty years.

Numbers ends with the Israelites entering the promised land, with Joshua taking leadership in place of Moses – who has been banned from the promised land due to disobedience.

Scripture to reflect on:

Numbers 6: 24-26

24 The LORD bless you and keep you;
25 the LORD make his face shine on you and be gracious to you;
26 the LORD turn his face toward you and give you peace

Deuteronomy

Author: Moses

Time Period: 1407 BC – 1406 BC

Key Themes / Outline: Moses and his three farewell speeches before his death.

Summary of the message:

Deuteronomy is very similar to Exodus, and is written as a reminder to the Israelites about the things God has done for them, and a reminder of what God expects from them. Moses blesses the tribes as he hands leadership over to Joshua, and dies on Mt. Nebo.

Scripture to reflect on:

Deuteronomy 32: 3-4

3 I will proclaim the name of the LORD. Oh, praise the greatness of our God!
4 He is the Rock, his works are perfect, and all his ways are just. A faithful God who does no wrong, upright and just is he.

Joshua

Author: Joshua (except for scriptures about his death)

Time Period: 1406 BC – 1375 BC

Key Themes / Outline: Narrative. Joshua commanding the armies that conquered much of the promised land of Canaan.

Summary of the message:

Joshua records the entry and conquest of the promised land, Joshua demonstrating his faith in God in being obedient and includes the battle of Jericho.

The land is divided up between the Israelites. Joshua dies, but on his death challenges the Israelites with *"Choose for yourselves today whom you will serve...as for me and my house, we will serve the LORD"* (24:15).

Scripture to reflect on:

Joshua 24:14

14 Now fear the LORD and serve him with all faithfulness. Throw away the gods your ancestors worshiped beyond the Euphrates River and in Egypt, and serve the LORD.

Judges

Author: Samuel, Nathan, Gad

Time Period: 1375 BC – 1075 BC

Key Themes / Outline: Mainly narrative, some poems. God establishing leaders called 'judges' to help rule and bring people back to God.

Summary of the message:

Judges reiterates that God is faithful, and will punish those who are unfaithful. Laws are set in place, and judges are assigned to implement and instruct on these. Israel slumps into moral demise, as their obedience only lasted as long as the life of that particular judge. Tribes had turned to idolization, and a civil war ensues, leaving only 600 men left in the tribe of Benjamin.

Scripture to reflect on:

Judges 3:12

> ¹² Again the Israelites did evil in the eyes of the LORD, and because they did this evil the LORD gave Eglon king of Moab power over Israel.

Ruth

Author: Samuel, Nathan, Gad

Time Period: 1140 BC

Key Themes / Outline: Narrative. The story of two widows, and their love and loyalty.

Summary of the message:

Ruth is a love story on many levels, and is written to demonstrate the love and faithfulness God has with us. After the death of her husband and sons, Naomi travels back to her homeland of Bethlehem, and her daughter in law Ruth stays loyal to her and travels with her. Ruth works in the fields of Naomi's relative Boaz, and he shows her favor. Boaz and Ruth are married and Ruth conceives a son named Obed, the grandfather of the great King David, in the lineage of Christ our Messiah.

Scripture to reflect on:

Ruth 1:16

[16] But Ruth replied, "Don't urge me to leave you or to turn back from you. Where you go I will go, and where you stay I will stay. Your people will be my people and your God my God.

1 Samuel

Author: Samuel, Nathan, Gad

Time Period: 1100 BC – 1010 BC

Key Themes / Outline: Narrative. Samuel appoints Israel's first king, Saul. After failure, Saul tries to prevent David from taking the throne.

Summary of the message:

Samuel was one of the last judges, and 1 Judges is written to illustrate how the Israelites chose a king, but abandoned God.

The Israelites are at war with the Philistines, and the Philistines capture the Ark of the Covenant. The Philistines are struck with fatal plagues, and return the Ark of the Covenant. Samuel appoints Saul as king, but after much trouble, God selects David to take over the throne.

A younger David slays the Giant Goliath, and Saul is jealous. Saul takes his own life later in the battlefield.

Scripture to reflect on:

1 Samuel 3:13

¹³ For I told him that I would judge his family forever because of the sin he knew about; his sons blasphemed God, and he failed to

restrain them.

2 Samuel

Author: Samuel, Nathan, Gad

Time Period: 1010 BC – 970 BC

Key Themes / Outline: Narrative. David brings the nation together, but after committing adultery and murder, suffers national and family failures.

Summary of the message:

2 Samuel tells the story of David. David ends up ruling the whole nation of Israel after the death of Ish-Bosheth. King David chooses to establish Jerusalem, and brings the Ark here. David sins during his reign, committing adultery with a married woman named Bethesda whom becomes pregnant, and then having her husband murdered. This affects the nation of Israel. The first baby dies, and another son child is born – Solomon – and he is the next King of Israel. David's other son, Absalom, plots a takeover, and David flees, before raising enough troops and restoring his title as King. Absalom is killed.

Scripture to reflect on:

2 Samuel 22:2-3

2 He said: "The LORD is my rock, my fortress and my deliverer;
3 my God is my rock, in whom I take refuge, my shield and the horn of my salvation. He is my stronghold, my refuge and my savior— from violent people you save me.

1 Kings

Author: Jeremiah

Time Period: 970 BC – 853 BC

Key Themes / Outline: Narrative and Prophecy. Solomon becomes the nest king, and on his death civil war tears apart the nation. Following kings are mostly bad. Elijah has confrontations with evil King Ahab.

Summary of the message:

1ˢᵗ Kings covers the reign of Solomon as the last king of Israel, and the kingdoms split after his death. Solomon starts building the temple his father David desired, and the Ark is brought there. Although Solomon was wise, he begins worshipping the gods of his wives, and he dies not long after.

Rehoboam takes over the kingdom and introduces high taxes, which results in a revolt from the Northern Tribes. Gods appoints Elijah to warn the evil King Ahab about idol worship.

Scripture to reflect on:

1 Kings 5:4-5

⁴ But now the LORD my God has given me rest on every side, and

there is no adversary or disaster. ⁵ I intend, therefore, to build a temple for the Name of the LORD my God, as the LORD told my father David, when he said, 'Your son whom I will put on the throne in your place will build the temple for my Name.'

2 Kings

Author: Jeremiah

Time Period: 852 BC – 586 BC

Key Themes / Outline: Narrative. Records the rulers of the divided kingdom. Israel is destroyed and Judah is conquered.

Summary of the message:

Jeremiah narrates the unfaithfulness and confusion of the Israelites, and how God uses his prophets to bring them hope.

Its purpose was to demonstrate the value of those who obey God, and the fate of those who refuse to obey and make Him ultimate ruler.

Elijah ends his ministry, and hands the task to Elisha, who follows Elijah's and Gods lead. Elijah dies, and Elisha continues his work, performing twice as many miracles.

Jeremiah also covers the details about the kings, who disobey God.

Scripture to reflect on:

2 Kings 19:10-11

[10] He replied, "I have been very zealous for the LORD God Almighty. The Israelites have rejected your covenant, torn down your altars, and put your prophets to death with the sword. I am the only one left, and now they are trying to kill me too."

[11] The LORD said, "Go out and stand on the mountain in the presence of the LORD, for the LORD is about to pass by."

Chronicles

Author: Ezra

Time Period: 1003 BC – 970 BC

Key Themes / Outline: Narrative. Genealogy. The bible's most complete genealogical record. Added events from the life of David.

Summary of the message:

1st Chronicles contains some similar stories as 2nd Samuel. It includes the genealogy from Adam through to Israel, the ancestry of the nation, and was written after the exile.

It reviews King Saul's death, David's reign and the preparation of the temple that Solomon would build.

Scripture to reflect on:

1 Chronicles 16:11-12

11 Look to the LORD and his strength; seek his face always.
12 Remember the wonders he has done, his miracles, and the judgments he pronounced

2 Chronicles

Author: Ezra

Time Period: 966 BC – 609 BC

Key Themes / Outline: Narrative history from Solomon's reign to captivity in Babylon.

Summary of the message:

2nd Chronicles outlines the blessings of the good kings, and exposes the sins of the bad kings. Written after the exile, it focuses on worshipping correctly. It also includes the wisdom of Solomon, and the construction of the temple. The latter chapters explain the split of the nation of Israel.

Scripture to reflect on:

2 Chronicles 12:12

¹² Because Rehoboam humbled himself, the LORD's anger turned

from him, and he was not totally destroyed. Indeed, there was some good in Judah.

Ezra

Author: Ezra

Time Period: 537 BC – 456 BC

Key Themes / Outline: Narrative history. Genealogy. The Jews are allowed to return to their homeland after being held captive in Babylon. Ezra leads as people rebuild the city.

Summary of the message:

Ezra outlines the return from exile in Babylon, and the events around rebuilding the temple in Jerusalem, which there is opposition to from surrounding enemies. The message that God is faithful to Jews resounds in this book with their return to Jerusalem.

Scripture to reflect on:

Ezra 3:3

3 Despite their fear of the peoples around them, they built the altar on its foundation and sacrificed burnt offerings on it to the Lord, both the morning and evening sacrifices.

Nehemiah

Author: Ezra and Nehemiah

Time Period: 445 BC – 432 BC

Key Themes / Outline: Narrative. Religious revival.

Summary of the message:

After the temple has been rebuilt, Nehemiah returns and concentrates on restoring the wall around Jerusalem for protection. The walls were built within a few weeks under the direction of Nehemiah, resulting in the enemies losing confidence.

Nehemiah joins Ezra in a religious revival. A renewal ceremony takes place, in which the public teaching of the law was explained. They understood that if they were to endure they must remember and follow God's Laws.

Scripture to reflect on:

Nehemiah 1:5-7

[5] Then I said:

"LORD, the God of heaven, the great and awesome God, who keeps his covenant of love with those who love him and keep his commandments, [6] let your ear be attentive and your eyes open to hear the prayer your servant is praying before your day and night for your servants, the people of Israel. I confess the sins we Israelites, including myself and my father's family, have committed against you.[7] We have acted very wickedly toward you. We have not obeyed the commands, decrees and laws you gave your servant Moses.

Esther

Author: Mordecai

Time Period: 483 BC – 456 BC

Key Themes / Outline: narrative history. Esther stops a plan to exterminate the Jews in Persia.

Summary of the message:

Esther, the queen of Persia who was personally chosen by the King saves her people. Most Jews returned to Jerusalem, and some stayed behind. Those that stayed were in danger of being exterminated after Mordecai refuses to bow down to Haman, infuriating him. Esther takes petition to the King, and as a result the King has Haman hung in the very gallows Haman built to kill the Jews.

Scripture to reflect on:

Esther 2:17

¹⁷ Now the king was attracted to Esther more than to any of the other women, and she won his favor and approval more than any of the other virgins. So he set a royal crown on her head and made her queen instead of Vashti.

Job

Author: Job (Moses may have compiled this book from Job's records)

Time Period: Before 2100 BC

Key Themes / Outline: Narrative history. Job suffers great personal tragedy, and asks "Why do people suffer?"

Summary of the message:

God allows Job to be directly attacked by Satan, resulting in him losing everything important to him. Even through this, Job remains faithful to God. Job's friends suggest his sufferings are due to his personal sins, although the message is that his faithfulness was being tested by God.

Job is restored, and is blessed with twice as much as he lost throughout his trials.

Scripture to reflect on:

Job 12: 10-13

10 In his hand is the life of every creature and the breath of all mankind.
11 Does not the ear test words as the tongue tastes food?
12 Is not wisdom found among the aged? Does not long life bring understanding?

13 "To God belong wisdom and power; counsel and understanding are his.

Psalm

Author: Mainly David, also Asaph, Ezra, the sons of Korah, Heman, Ethan, Moses and other unnamed authors

Time Period: 1407 BC – 586 BC

Key Themes / Outline: Prayers and hymns representing a personal model of how to relate to God.

Summary of the message:

The Psalms include praises of joy, laments, blessings, and thanksgivings. They are directed at God and they help us to express and communicate ourselves to Him, with our joy and our pain in everyday life.

We read about the Psalmist's emotions from one extreme to another, from praising, appreciating and worshiping God with fervor, to regret and crying out to Him in anguish.

Scripture to reflect on:

Psalm 23:1-6

1 The LORD is my shepherd, I lack nothing.

2 He makes me lie down in green pastures, he leads me beside quiet

waters,

3 he refreshes my soul. He guides me along the right paths for his name's sake.

4 Even though I walk through the darkest valley, I will fear no evil, for you are with me; your rod and your staff, they comfort me.

5 You prepare a table before me in the presence of my enemies. You anoint my head with oil; my cup overflows.

6 Surely your goodness and love will follow me all the days of my life, and I will dwell in the house of the LORD forever.

Proverbs

Author: Solomon, Verses 30 and 31 by Agur and Lemuel

Time Period: 950 BC

Key Themes / Outline: Proverbs. Parables. Poetry. Offers advice on various areas of life, encouraging wise living.

Summary of the message:

Proverbs teaches wisdom to Gods people. A wise man and a foolish man are often compared. The message of working for your rewards is often stated.

The finishing chapters give wisdom to leaders, and give instruction for living a Godly life.

Scripture to reflect on:

Proverbs 24:3-4

3 By wisdom a house is built, and through understanding it is established;
4 through knowledge its rooms are filled with rare and beautiful treasures.

Ecclesiastes

Author: Solomon

Time Period: 937 BC

Key Themes / Outline: Autobiographical story. Life without God leads to meaningless and despair.

Summary of the message:

Solomon has seen the errors of his ways, and writes to spare the misery for future generations who may seek materialistic things and selfish pleasures instead of God. It teaches wisdom through his personal experiences, and encourages living a meaningful life.

Scripture to reflect on:

Ecclesiastes 12:13

13 The conclusion, when all has been heard, is: Fear God and keep His commandments, because this applies to every person.

Song of Solomon

Author: Solomon (although this is debated)

Time Period: 950 BC

Key Themes / Outline: A poem celebrating romantic love, also reflecting how God loves us.

Summary of the message:

Song of Solomon is a love story between a bridegroom and his bride. It covers courtship and the sanctity of marriage. It demonstrates the love God has for us, his people.

Scripture to reflect on:

Song of Solomon 4:6-7

6 Until the day breaks and the shadows flee, I will go to the mountain of myrrh and to the hill of incense.
7 You are altogether beautiful, my darling; there is no flaw in you.

Isaiah

Author: Isaiah

Time Period: 739 BC – 701 BC

Key Themes / Outline: Narrative history. Looks at the failures of the nations, and prophecies about the coming of Jesus.

Summary of the message:

Isaiah was written to call Gods people back to faithfulness. He declares punishment for the sins of the North and South Kingdoms, as well as the surrounding nations. It speaks of the restoration after the return from Babylon, and foretells of the coming of Christ, who will bring new life in His death. It finished describing the great reward for those who are faithful and trust God.

Scripture to reflect on:

Isaiah 53:4-5

4 Surely he took up our pain and bore our suffering, yet we considered him punished by God, stricken by him, and afflicted.
5 But he was pierced for our transgressions, he was crushed for our

iniquities; the punishment that brought us peace was on him, and by his wounds we are healed.

Jeremiah

Author: Jeremiah

Time Period: 627 BC – 586 BC

Key Themes / Outline: Prophetic Oracle. Narrative History. A message that people need to turn back to God. Jeremiah speaks to Judah before Babylon destroys the nation.

Summary of the message:

The purpose of Jeremiah was to warn of the devastation that they were about to face and to urge Judah to return and yield to God. Jeremiah was a priest who God calls to be His prophet. Jeremiah identifies their sins, as he wants them to understand the serious condition of their sinful ways. He then gives prophecies of the coming king and the New Covenant that would be made. God promises to rescue his people

Scripture to reflect on:

Jeremiah 17:7-8

7 But blessed is the one who trusts in the LORD, whose confidence is in him.
8 They will be like a tree planted by the water that sends out its roots by the stream. It does not fear when heat comes; its leaves are always green. It has no worries in a year of drought and never fails to bear fruit.

Lamentations

Author: Jeremiah

Time Period: 586 BC

Key Themes / Outline: Five poems of sorrow for the fallen nation of Jerusalem.

Summary of the message:

Lamentations contains sorrowful songs and poems, written after the destruction of Jerusalem by the Babylonians, with the intent to teach Gods people that disobedience results in despair.

Scripture to reflect on:

Lamentations 5:19

19 'You, Lord, reign forever; your throne endures from generation to generation.'

Ezekiel

Author: Ezekiel

Time Period: 593 BC – 585 BC

Key Themes / Outline: Narrative History. Ezekiel speaks to the Jews who were captive in Babylon.

Summary of the message:

Ezekiel announces judgement on Judah, with the chance to repent. Ezekiel receives visions that confront the sinful nation. He tells parables, one comparing Israel to an adulterous woman. It ends with a message of restoration and deliverance through God.

Scripture to reflect on:

Ezekiel 2:3

I am sending you to the sons of Israel, to a rebellious people who have rebelled against Me; they and their fathers have transgressed against Me to this very day.

Daniel

Author: Daniel

Time Period: 605 BC – 539 BC

Key Themes / Outline: Narrative history. Daniel becomes Prime Minister even though he is captive in Babylon. Obedience under pressure.

Summary of the message:

Daniel covers the events of the Babylonian captivity, and apocalyptic visions given by God, revealing Gods plans for everyone's future. It includes Daniels own story of captivity, working as a slave for the Babylonian King Nebuchadnezzar, where Daniel and his friends often stood for Godliness rather than the accepted culture. They were thrown into a fiery furnace for not bowing to the Kings idol, but survived. Daniel ended up interpreting the Kings dreams and was promoted to chief over the wise men in Babylon.

The purpose of this book is to provide a historical account how the Lord God protected and provided for His faithful followers while in captivity. It also includes a vision of future redemption and hope.

Scripture to reflect on:

Daniel 4:3

3 How great are his signs, how mighty his wonders! His kingdom is an eternal kingdom; his dominion endures from generation to generation.

Hosea

Author: Hosea

Time Period: 753 BC

Key Themes / Outline: narrative History. Prophetic Oracle. Israel being unfaithful to God, just as Hosea's wife was unfaithful to him.

Summary of the message:

Hosea bring the message of spiritual adultery to the sinful Northern Kingdom, and illustrates Gods unlimited love for his people who were active in enslaving the poor and bowing to idols. God sends an opportunity for the Northern Kingdom to repent, but they end up in long-lasting captivity.

God instructs Hosea to marry a disloyal woman, Gomer, and he obeys. She is unfaithful and leaves him for another man. He finds her, forgives her and takes her home. This is to illustrate how God wants to be with his people.

Scripture to reflect on:

Hosea 3:3

3 The LORD said to me, "Go, show your love to your wife again, though she is loved by another man and is an adulteress. Love her as the LORD loves the Israelites, though they turn to other gods and love the sacred raisin cakes.

OLD TESTAMENT

Joel

Author: Joel

Time Period: 853 BC

Key Themes / Outline: Narrative. Prophetic Oracle. Foretelling of Gods judgement on Judah.

Summary of the message:

The intention of Joel was to encourage the Southern Kingdom to repent, or prepare for imminent judgement. He compares the judgement of God to a plague of locusts. God is waiting and promises deliverance and restoration of the land.

Scripture to reflect on:

Joel 2:12-13

12 Return to Me with all your heart, and with fasting, weeping and mourning; And rend your heart and not your garments.

13 Now return to the Lord your God, for He is gracious and compassionate, slow to anger, abounding in lovingkindness and relenting of evil.

Amos

Author: Amos

Time Period: 766 BC

Key Themes / Outline: God will judge the prosperous for not helping the poor.

Summary of the message:

Amos is to present Gods judgement on the Northern Kingdom, and calls them to repent. He suggests that although the people are religious, it is superficial. He warns of the coming judgement.

The purpose of the book of Amos was to announce God's holy judgment on the Kingdom of Israel (the Northern Kingdom), call them to repentance, and to turn from their self-righteous sins and idolatry. God raised up the prophet Amos, as an act of His great mercy to a people who repeatedly shunned and disobeyed Him.

Scripture to reflect on:

Amos 5:14

14 Seek good and not evil, that you may live; and thus may the LORD God of hosts be with you, just as you have said!

Obadiah

Author: Obadiah

Time Period: 853 BC

Key Themes / Outline: Prophetic Oracle. Warnings to Edom, a nation bordering Judah.

Summary of the message:

Obadiah is the shortest book in the Old testament, and uses Edom as an example of how God will judge all of those who are against His people.

Scripture to reflect on:

Obadiah 1:8

8 In the loftiness of your dwelling place, who say in your heart, 'Who will bring me down to earth?' He proclaims God's judgment on Edom, 'Will I not on that day,' declares the LORD, 'Destroy wise men from Edom and understanding from the mountain of Esau?'

Jonah

Author: Jonah

Time Period: 760 BC

Key Themes / Outline: narrative History. Prophetic Oracle. Jonah goes to Nineveh, and finds Israel's enemies receptive to Gods message.

Summary of the message:

Jonah illustrates Gods patience with the sinful city of Nineveh job was appointed to send a message from God, and originally ran from Him by boarding a ship to Tarshis. A great storm developed, and job explained that it was the wrath of God due to his disobedience, so they threw him overboard, where he was swallowed by an enormous fish. Three days later, God had the fish cough him up, and job obeyed by going to Nineveh to preach the message of repentance. The sinful city repented.

Scripture to reflect on:

Jonah 4:2

2 knew that You are a gracious and compassionate God, slow to anger and abundant in lovingkindness, and one who relents concerning calamity.

Micah

Author: Micah

Time Period: 735 BC

Key Themes / Outline: Prophetic Oracle. Corruption is exposed. A promise of restoration and forgiveness for Gods people.

Summary of the message:

Micah is written as a warning to the Northern and Southern Kingdoms, describing the judgement that would fall on them that would eventually exile the nation. He also predicts the birthplace of the messiah in Bethlehem, telling that He is an infinite savior.

Scripture to reflect on:

Micah 7:18

18 Who is a God like You, who pardons iniquity and passes over the rebellious act of the remnant of His possession? He does not retain His anger forever, because He delights in unchanging love.

Nahum

Author: Nahum

Time Period: 697 BC

Key Themes / Outline: Prophetic Oracle. Nahum foretells Nineveh's destruction.

Summary of the message:

Nineveh returned to wickedness shortly after job's visit, and Nahum gives them a final warning of judgement. They disregard Nahum's message and Nineveh is destroyed within fifty years.

Scripture to reflect on:

Nahum 1:12

12 Though they are at full strength and likewise many, even so, they will be cut off and pass away. Though I have afflicted you, I will afflict you no longer.

Habakkuk

Author: Habakkuk

Time Period: 625 BC

Key Themes / Outline: Narrative History. Prophetic Oracle. Dialogue with God, discussing problems of suffering and justice.

Summary of the message:

Habakkuk is a short book, and carries God's message to His people. Habakkuk describes the sin of earlier day Judah, and asks God why evil is prevailing. God answers, and urges His people to be patient.

Scripture to reflect on:

Habakkuk 3:2

2 LORD, I have heard the report about You and I fear. O LORD, revive Your work in the midst of the years, in the midst of the years make it known; in wrath remember mercy.

Zephaniah

Author: Zephaniah

Time Period: 520 BC

Key Themes / Outline: Focusing on the coming 'Day of the Lord'.

Summary of the message:

Written just before the fall of Judah in the Southern Kingdom. God appointed the prophet Zephaniah to spread the message of impending judgement, and the call to repent. Zephaniah writes about a day of hope, demonstrating God giving sinners more than they deserve.

Scripture to reflect on:

Zephaniah 1:7

[7] Be silent before the Sovereign LORD, for the day of the LORD is near.
The LORD has prepared a sacrifice; he has consecrated those he has invited.

Haggai

Author: Haggai

Time Period: 520 BC

Key Themes / Outline: Narrative History. Prophetic Oracle. A reminder to put God first.

Summary of the message:

God called Haggai to encourage the people to complete the building of the temple, which had ceased construction due to opposition from neighboring countries causing fear in the Jews.

Scripture to reflect on:

Haggai 2:5

5 As for the promise which I made you when you came out of Egypt, My Spirit is abiding in your midst; do not fear!

Zechariah

Author: Zechariah

Time Period: 520 BC

Key Themes / Outline: Narrative History. Urging Jews to work on the temple.

Summary of the message:

Zechariah wrote to the remainder of the Jews who had recently returned from exile, and needed to conform to the law of God again. He also writes about judgement on neighboring enemies.

Scripture to reflect on:

Zechariah 14:4

4 In that day His feet will stand on the Mount of Olives, which is in front of Jerusalem on the east; and the Mount of Olives will be split in its middle from east to west by a very large valley, so that half of the mountain will move toward the north and the other half toward the south.

Malachi

Author: Malachi

Time Period: 430 BC

Key Themes / Outline: Prophetic Oracle. To stir the people to turn back to God.

Summary of the message:

Malachi was written after the return from Babylon, and is written to ensure the hearts of the Jews were right with God. He explains the coming judgement, and God's fiery judgment. He prophesies that God will send a messenger to prepare the way (John the Baptist).

Scripture to reflect on:

Malachi 3:1

3 Behold, I am going to send My messenger, and he will clear the way before Me. And the Lord, whom you seek, will suddenly come to His temple; and the messenger of the covenant, in whom you delight, behold, He is coming," says the LORD of hosts.

OLD TESTAMENT

JOSEPH KNOWLE

Made in the USA
Coppell, TX
03 January 2024

27240047R00036